MACRAMÉ FOR BEGINNERS

The Complete Macramé Guide with Step-by-Step Knots Instructions. Choose Your Favorites DIY Jewelry and Bracelets Projects, and Create Wall Hangings and Plant Hangers Patterns for Your Home Decor

Veronica Wilson

TABLE OF CONTENTS

INTRODUCTION

Macramé is an intricate weaving technique with roots in South America and Africa. It looks difficult, but it requires little more than a couple of basic knots to get started.

This book will teach you how to create various macramé projects. With these simple techniques under your belt, you'll be able to whip up something for yourself or your friends in no time at all.

If you are not familiar with the name macramé, the term is derived from the French word "macarrier," which means to tie together. This is how it got its name—tying together different strings of material was how the craft started centuries ago, just as weaving was an ancient method of making fabrics.

Macramé works well for a beginner because it requires only rope and knots. There's no needlework involved, no sewing on buttons or gathering tulle/netting/ribbon/fringe/etc. It's all done by tying your knot—creating a loop in one end of your rope or cord and then wrapping and weaving that cord around something else using knots as anchors.

Macramé materials are fairly easy to find, but they are not the easiest things in the world to work with—they are slippery and hard to hold on to. A knotted cord is thick enough to fray over time, so if you use it, you will probably have to replace it every 2–3 years. The knotting process itself can sometimes be frustrating, especially if it's your first time working with that type of material/knotting. You may end up untangling the cord from itself or getting knots out of the way so you can continue weaving your project. (Don't worry—I've got solutions for all these problems).

This book will also provide the basic techniques for working with macramé cord, step-by-step instructions for doing the projects, and tips to help you get through all these difficulties.

You can make macramé in several ways—the two most common are knotting and weaving. The knots use one kind of cord, while weaving uses braided or knotted material. Both methods of working involve knots, but bindings from tying off one piece of material to another as well as simple looping techniques are also used in both.

Anchoring the pieces of material together is very important in macramé. You can't just weave a cord around the pieces and expect a nice finish.

When making macramé, there are two types of knots you will encounter:

Plain knots (butterfly knot, square knot, and arbor knot): these are the most basic knots. They are beautiful and create fairly durable knots. If you are going to knot something by hand rather than using a cord/string/Marcella rope with no natural fiber content (resistant to fraying), these should be your knot type of choice. They are also good to use when making a series of knots in one string.

Plaited knots: these knots look like braids and are particularly useful for heavy materials, such as leather or thicker rope. Plaited knots also hold up better to wear-and-tear (e.g., rubbing against clothes or furniture) because more strands of material are secured in the knot rather than two end pieces that can fray and break off over time with wear and tear.

Learn more as you progress through the stages of learning this craft, and you will find that your experience with macramé rapidly improves, resulting in beautiful pieces you can be proud of.

CHAPTER 1. MACRAMÉ TOOLBOX

MACRAMÉ SUPPLIES

Macramé stylists make use of different types of materials. Materials can be classified into two major categories: natural materials and synthetic materials.

Natural Materials

The qualities of natural materials differ from synthetic materials, and knowing these qualities would help you to make better use of them. Natural cord materials existing today include jute, hemp, leather, cotton, silk, and flax. There are also yarns made from natural fibers. Natural material fibers are made from plants and animals.

Synthetic Materials

As natural materials, synthetic materials are also used in macramé projects. The fibers of synthetic materials are made through chemical processes. The major ones are nylon beading cord, olefin, satin cord, and parachute cord.

CORD MEASUREMENT

Before embarking on a macramé project, it is essential that you determine how much rope you will need. This includes knowing the length of the required cord and the total number of materials you have to purchase.

Equipment: To measure, you will need paper for writing, a pencil, a tape rule, and a calculator. You would also need some basic knowledge of unit conversion as shared below:

- 1 inch = 25.4 millimeters = 2.54 centimeters

- 1 foot = 12 inches
- 1 yard = 3 feet = 36 inches
- 1 yard = 0.9 meters

Note: The circumference of a ring = 3.14 * diameter measured across the ring.

MEASURING WIDTH

The first thing to do is to determine the finished width of the widest area of your project. Once you have this width, pencil it down.

Next, determine the actual size of the materials by measuring their width from edge to edge.

You can then proceed to determine the type of knot pattern you wish to use with the knowledge of the knot pattern. You must know the width and spacing (if required) of each knot. You should also determine if you want to add more cords to widen an area or if you would need extra cords for damps.

With the formula given above, calculate and determine the circumference of the ring of your designs.

Determine the mounting technique to be used. The cord can be mounted to a dowel, ring, or other cord. Bent cords affect both the length and width of the cord measurement.

CORD PREPARATION

Although it is not often emphasized, the preparation of cords and their preparation for use in macramé projects is one of the fundamental pillars of the art of macramé. At times, specialized processes such as conditioning and stiffening of cords need to be carried out before macramé projects can be begun. In general, however, cord preparation in macramé is mainly concerned with dealing with cut ends and preventing these ends from unraveling during the project. During a project, constant handling of materials can distort the ends, which can end up having disastrous consequences on your project. Before starting your project, if you do not appropriately prepare special kinds of cords, like ones that were made by the twisting of individual strands, that cord is likely to come apart, effectively destroying your project completely.

Therefore, cord preparation is extremely and incomparably important to the success of any macramé project; the preparation of each cord is meant to be done during the first step of making any knot, which is the step where you cut out your desired length of cord from the larger piece.

For cord conditioning, experts recommend rubbing beeswax along the length of the cord. To condition your cord, simply get a bit of beeswax, let it warm up a bit in your hands, and rub it along the cord's length. This will help prevent unwanted tight curls on your cord. Note that beeswax may be applied to both natural and synthetic materials. However, in the case of synthetic materials, only satin and fine nylon cords require mandatory conditioning. After conditioning, inspect your cords for any imperfections and discard useless pieces to ensure the perfection of your project. After conditioning then comes the actual process of cord preparation. Cords can be prepared (i.e., the ends can be prevented from fraying) through the use of a flame, a knot, tape, and glue.

To prevent unraveling of your cord using a flame, first test a small piece of the material with the flame from a small lighter. The material needs to melt, not burn. If it burns, then such a cord is not suitable for flame preparation. To prepare using a flame, simply hold the cord to the tip of the flame for 2 to 5 seconds, make sure the cord does not ignite but melts. Flame preparation is suitable for cords made from olefin, polyester, and nylon, and the process is compulsory for the preparation of parachute cords.

Tying knots at the end of the cord is another effective method to prevent fraying. The overhand knot is an all-time favorite, but some knots are best suited to flexible cords, can be used if you think the knot might have to be undone at some point in your project. The Stevedore knot can be used to prevent fraying when using slippery materials.

Glue is another priceless alternative that can be used to prevent fraying at the ends of cords efficiently. However, not all kinds of glue may be used in cord preparation. Only certain brands, such as the Alien's Stop Fray™, may be used in cord preparation. Household glue might also be used, but only when diluted with water. To prepare your cord, simply rub the glue on the ends of the material and leave it to dry. If you intend to pass beads over the glued end, roll the cord's end between your fingers to make it narrower as it dries. Nail polish may also be used as an alternative to glue.

Simply wrap the tape around the end of the cord where you want to prevent the fraying of your material. Make sure the end of the cord remains narrow by squeezing it between your fingers. It is advisable to use masking tape or cellophane tape for your preparations.

A special class of macramé cords, known as a parachute cord, requires a special form of preparation. To prepare a parachute cord, pull out the core yarns from the sleeve, and expose the yarns by about half an inch. Now cut the core yarns back so that they become even with the outer sleeve, and then push the sleeve forward till the yarns become invisible. To complete the preparation, apply flame to the outer sleeve till it melts, and then press the handle of your lighter onto the sleeve while it's still warm to flatten the area and keep it closed up. The melted area will look darker and more plastic than the rest of the material.

FINISHING TECHNIQUES

Finishing techniques refer to the methods by which the ends of cords after knots have been created may be taken care of to give a neat and tidy project. Finishing is often referred to as tying off. Several finishing knots are available and are extremely effective methods for executing finishing processes. Reliable finishing knots include the overhand knot and the barrel knot.

Folding techniques are also reliable finishing techniques. For flexible materials like cotton, all you need to do is fold the ends flat against the back surface and add glue to the ends to hold them in place. For less flexible materials, fold the cords to the back, then pass them under a loop from one or more knots, and then apply glue, allow it to dry, and cut off excess material.

Finally, you can do your finishing with the aid of fringes. You may choose between a brushed fringe and a beaded fringe.

DIFFERENCE BETWEEN A STRING, A ROPE AND A CORD

Macramé string is the smooth single twist string that Niroma Studio started working with as it is known today.

String stretches faster than string or thread because it unwinds quickly such that the total width will range from 1 to 1.5 mm from when firmly wounded along the conduit to when splitting and breathable. Other retailers can mark something special, so keep that in mind.

"What's the right macramé string for beginners?" I always get questioned, and I always choose the 5 mm natural cotton string. It is the right size to hang a nice medium-sized wall, and it fits better than the 3 mm; plus, it has a very compact medium twist on it, and it can be gently unknotted and reknitted a couple of times before losing its credibility as long as you are conscious. And being gentle on the hands, of course, always tends to keep you moving!

Macramé rope is typically a 3-strand rope where the fibers are wrapped around each other (sometimes called a 3-ply). I saw it in four strands, but traditional rope appears to be three strands. Macramé rope is usually stronger than macramé string, and it gives you a nice, wavy fringe when you untwist it, so it's perfect for adding dimension to your job.

Since it is heavier, I like to use it for parts of items that would have to carry considerable weight. Macramé rope often stretches when it has been cut, so depending on where you stay, how much humidity you have, etc., it will also stretch up to 1 cm. Macramé rope is typically a 6-strand (or more) braided thread, or what I believe was more widely used for macramé in the 1970s, so early 1980s when the cotton string wasn't exactly 'the thing' to use. The tightly woven cotton macramé rope is sometimes called "sash rope." Sash rope is a little rigid to use and quite hard to remove, yet it's incredibly solid, so it's perfect for weight-bearing parts and if you're trying to add plenty of strength to your job. In my experience, Macramé rope is the worst on hands, but when you want a certain look or versatility, there's no discomfort, no cost!

Then there is polypropylene (or polyolefin) macramé rope; some of you may recognize one labeled variant as Bonnie Design String, which is perfect for outdoor usage because it does not shape because easily as cotton. The edge can be "frizzy," and that's only something to hold in mind.

TOOLS REQUIRED FOR MACRAMÉ

Macramé Project Board

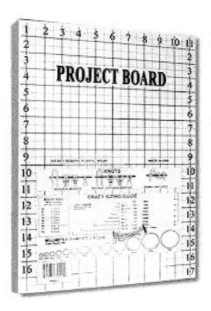

A project mounting board is a principal device required for macramé. The board is the working area where it secures the work. At art shops, you can find boards with grid-inch markings and fitting directions written on the fronts. A project board may, therefore, be rendered by gluing together or using cork foam sheets. The board may be suitable for a macramé project, so long as it is thick enough to prevent the nails from sticking out the back.

T-Nails

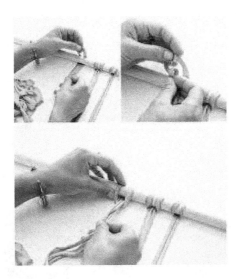

T-Nails are used to secure onto the mounting board the macramé yarn or rope. T-nails come out in various sizes. Smaller nails are ideal for smaller, more delicate designs. Nails appear to break follow prolonged wing use. Those built of steel are more durable and can maintain for longer use.

Pattern

Many things can be created with macramé—from purses to infant mobiles. A handy tool is a macramé template. Macramé patterns provide step-by-step guidance on the knots to be used, directions for calculating, and guidelines for final assembly. Buy patterns, or you will search them online.

Scissors

A decent pair of sharp scissors could be used to cut threads correctly on a macramé layout. There are different sizes and comfort grips. Consider purchasing the sort to cover the blades with a sheath protector.

Tweezers

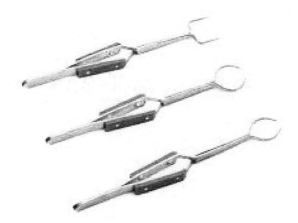

Another device used for the decoration function is tweezers. You can use a pair of tweezers to help good knot threads between the beadwork.

Needles

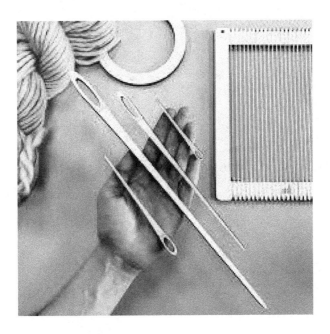

Needles are used for macramé. Needles are used for the alignment of the completed product and perforation. Depending on the inclination are used blunt-end or tapestry needles and Chenille or pointed needles. Specific measurements are used to fit yarn styles like silk or nylon and for different formed beads.

CHAPTER 2. MACRAMÉ BASIC KNOTS

LARK'S HEAD KNOT

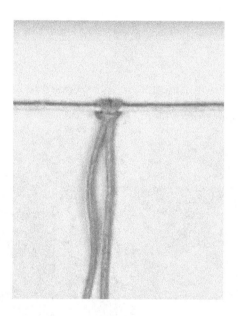

This is a boundless foundation knot for any venture and can be used as the foundation of the project. Use a lightweight cord for this; it can be purchased at craft stores or online wherever you get your macramé supplies.

Watch the photos very carefully as you move along with this project, and take your time to ensure you are with the correct string at the correct point of the project.

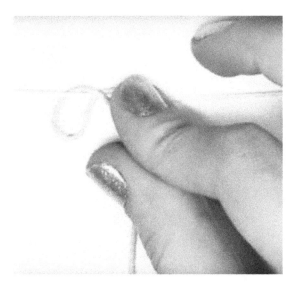

Use the base string as the core part of the knot, working around the end of the string with the cord. Make sure all is even as you loop the string around the base of the cord.

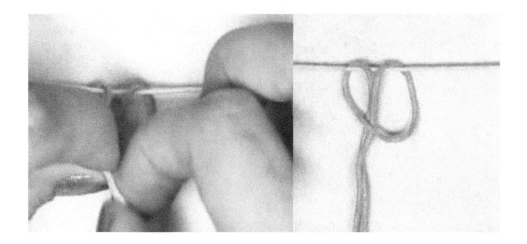

Create a slipknot around the base of the string and keep both ends even as you pull the cord through the center of the piece.

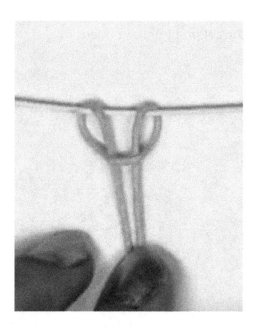

For the finished project, make sure that you have all your knots secure and firm throughout, and ensure it is all even. It is going to take practice before you can get it perfectly each time, but remember that practice does make perfect, and with time, you are going to get it without too much trouble.

Make sure all is even and secure and tie off. Snip off all the loose ends, and you are ready to go!

REVERSE LARK'S HEAD KNOT

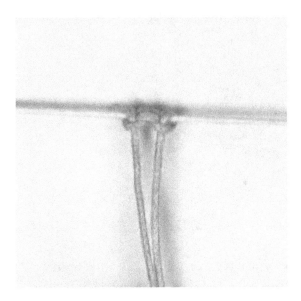

This is a great beginning knot and can be used as the foundation of the project. Use a lightweight cord for this; this again can be purchased at craft stores or online wherever you get your macramé supplies.

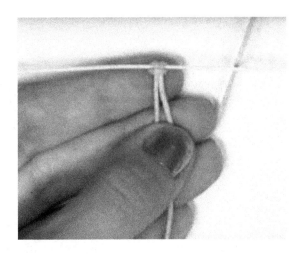

Do not rush and ensure you have even tension throughout. Practice makes perfect, but with the illustrations to help you, you will find it is not hard at all to create.

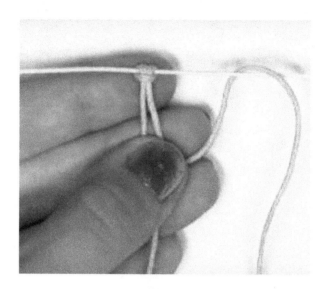

Use two hands to make sure that you have everything even and tight as you work. You can use tweezers if it helps to make it tight against the base of the string.

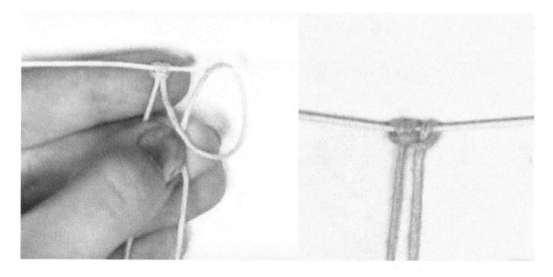

Utilize both hands to pull the string evenly down against the base string to create the knot.

Once more, keep the base even as you pull the center, creating the firm knot against your guide cord.

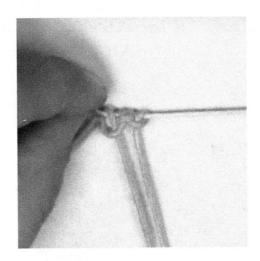

CAPUCHIN KNOT

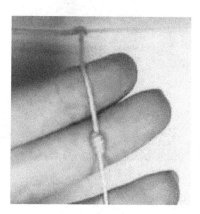

This knot for any project and can be used as the foundation of the project. Use a lightweight cord for this.

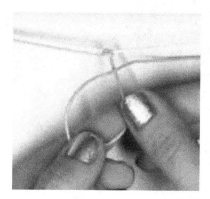

Watch the photos very carefully as you move along with this project, and take your time to ensure you are using the correct string at the right point of the project.

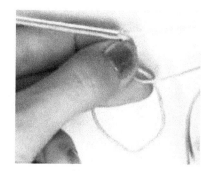

Start at the base cord, tying the knot in it, and work your way down the length of the project.

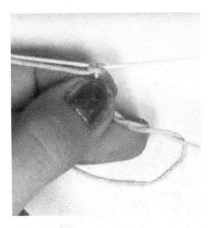

Twist the cord around itself two times, pulling the string through the center to form the knot.

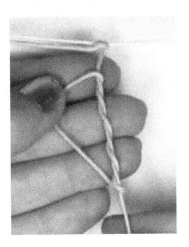

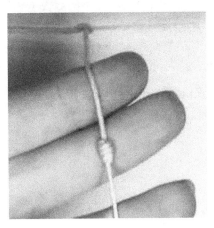

Make sure all is even and secure and tie off. Snip off all the loose ends, and you are ready to go!

CROWN KNOT

This is a great beginning knot and can be used as the foundation of the project. Use a lightweight cord for this.

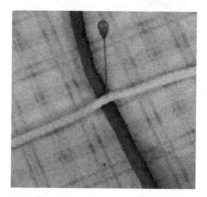

Never rush, then make sure you have even tension throughout. Practice makes perfect, but with the illustrations to help you, you will find it is not hard at all to create.

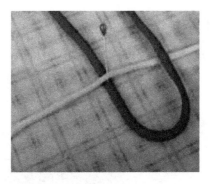

Use a pin to help keep everything in place as you are working.

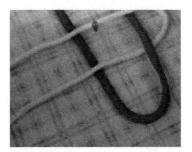

Weave the strings in and out of each other, as you can see in the photos. It helps to practice with different colors, to help you see what is going on.

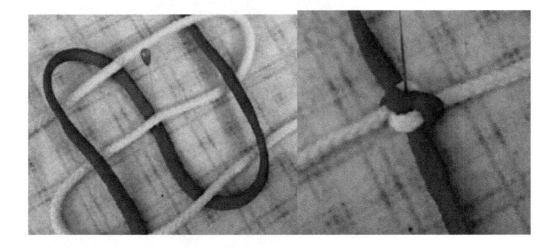

Pull the knot tight, then repeat for the next row on the outside.

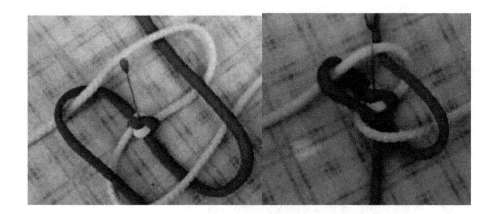

Stay to do this as often as you like to create the knot. You can make it as thick as you like, depending on the project. You can also create more than one length on the same cord.

DIAGONAL DOUBLE HALF-KNOT

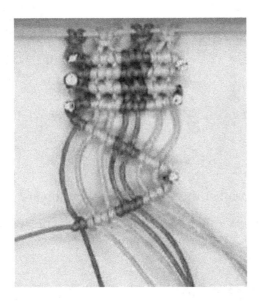

This is the seamless knot to use for decorations, basket hangings, or any projects that are going to require you to put weight on the project. Use a heavier weight cord for this, which you can find at craft stores or online.

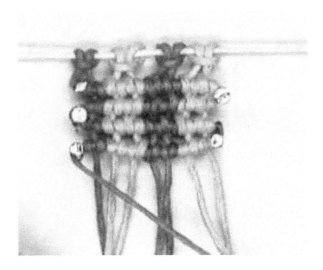

Do not rush, also make sure you have even tension throughout. Practice makes perfect, but with the illustrations to help you, you will find it is not hard at all to create.

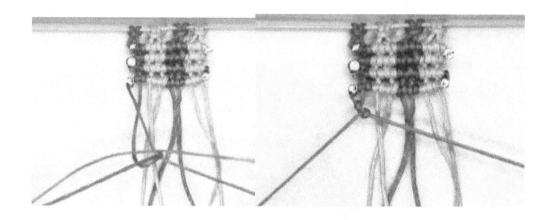

Twitch at the uppermost of the project then work your way toward the bottom. Keep it even as you work your way throughout the piece. Tie the knots at 4-inch intervals, working your way down the entire thing.

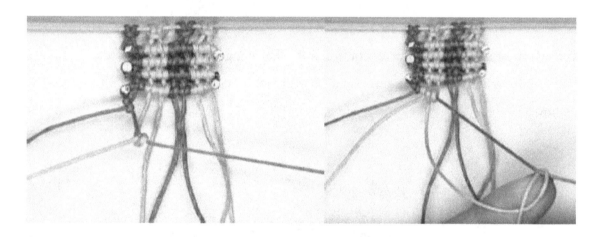

Weave in and out throughout, watching the photo as you can see for the right placement of the knots. Again, it helps to practice with different colors, so you can see what you need to do throughout the piece.

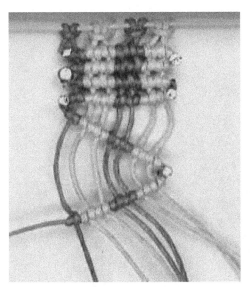

FRIVOLITE KNOT

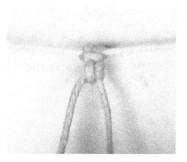

This can be used as the foundation for the base of the project. Use a lightweight cord for this too. It can be bought at craft stores or online.

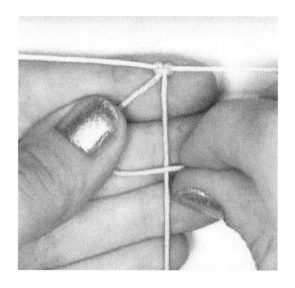

No need to rush, and make sure you have even tension throughout. With the illustrations to help you, you may find it is not hard at all to create.

Use the base string as the guide to hold it in place, then tie the knot onto this. This is a very straightforward knot; look at the photo and follow the directions you see.

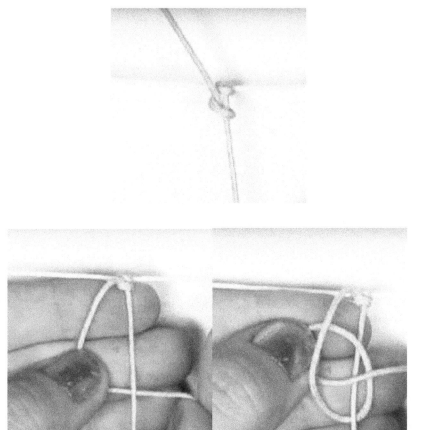

Pull the end of the cord up and through the center.

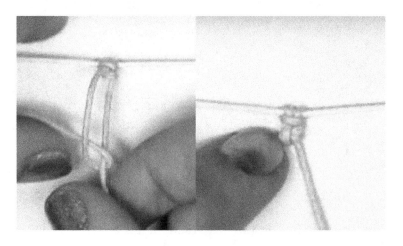

When done, make sure that you have all your knots secure and firm throughout, and ensure it is all even. Make sure all is even and secure and tie off. Snip off all the loose ends.

HORIZONTAL DOUBLE HALF-KNOT

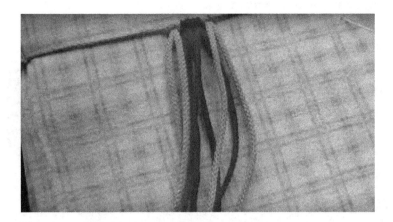

It can be used as the foundation for the base of the project. Use a lightweight cord for this by purchasing from wherever you get your macramé supplies.

Follow the photos very carefully and take your time to make sure you are using the correct string at each point of the project.

Make sure you have even tension throughout. Practice makes perfect, but with the illustrations to help you, you will find it is not hard at all to create.

Twitch at the uppermost of the project, then work your way toward the bottom. Keep it even as you work your way throughout the piece. Tie the knots at 4-inch intervals, working your way down the entire item.

Once finished, make sure that you have all your knots secure and firm throughout, and do your best to make sure it is all even. Make sure all is even and secure, and tie and snip off all the loose ends.

JOSEPHINE KNOT

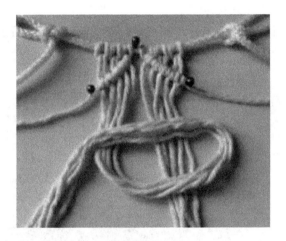

This is the ideal knot to use for decorations, basket hangings, or any projects that are going to require you to put weight on the project. Use a heavier weight cord for this, which you can find at craft stores or online.

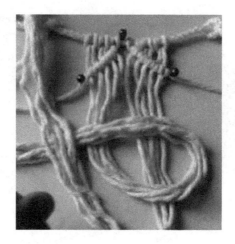

Follow the photos very carefully as you move along with this project. Take your time to correctly move the cords. Do not rush, and make sure the cords have even tension throughout.

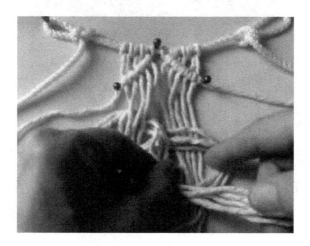

Use the pins along with the knots that you have tied, and work with larger areas simultaneously. This is going to help you keep the project in place as you continue to work throughout the piece.

Pull the ends of the knots through the loops and form the ring at the center of the strings.

If you are done, make sure that your knots are secure and firm, making sure they are all even. It is going to take practice before you can get it perfectly.

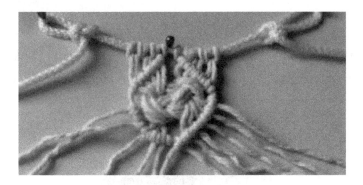

Make sure all is even and secure and tie off. Snip off all the loose ends.

CHAPTER 3. MORE MACRAMÉ BASIC KNOTS

CHINESE CROWN KNOT

This can be used as the foundation for the base of the project. Use lightweight cord for this—it can be purchased at craft stores or online wherever you get your macramé supplies. Do not rush, and make sure you have even tension throughout. Practice makes perfect, but with the illustrations to help you, you will find it is not hard at all to create. Use a pin to help keep everything in place while you are working. Weave the strings in and out of each other, as you can see in the photos. It helps to practice with different colors to help you see what is going on. Pull the knot tight, then repeat for the row on the outside.

Continue to do this as often as you like to create the knot. You can make it as thick as you like, depending on the project. You can also create more than one length on the same cord.

HALF KNOTS AND SQUARE KNOTS

One of the most commonly used macramé knots is a square knot, and it can also be generated as a left or a right-facing knot. The half-knot is actually half a knot in a rectangle. This may be left or right facing; it entirely depends on which side you work from.

Square knots require at least four cords (two active cords and two filler strings) but may provide more. The operating strings are the first and the last ones. We will name them to string one and string four in operation. The cables in the center are filler cables, so we're going to list those two and three. Such cords swap locations but still maintain their initial numbering.

A square knot (left facing) on the left side of the completed knot has a vertical hump. Take your first cord (operational cord one) and pass it over the middle cords (filler cords two and three) to the right and under your final cord (operational cord 4). Take operational cord four and shift it under all filler cords and over operational cord one to the west. Push all operating cords to close, leaving cords parallel to the filler. It is a half-square knot faced to the west. Functional cords currently swapped places on the right with functional cord one and operating cord four on the left. Taking running cord one and pass it over the two filler cords to the left and under operating cord four. Take functioning cord four and shift it under all filler strings and overworking cord one to the right. Pull and tie all active strings. Hold cables straight on the material. It completes the square knot to the left side.

A half-knot and square knot facing the right side of the completed knot has a vertical hump. Remove the last cord (cord four) and transfer it over the filler cords (strings two and three) and under the first cord (cord one) to the west. Take working cord one and push it under the filler cords and overworking cord four to the center. Pull and lock all strings, making it clear. That is a half-square knot facing right. Functional cords now have positions swapped, and working cord one is on the right and working cord four on the left. Take work cord four over to the side, over the cords of the filler, and underworking cord one. Take job cord one and shift it to the west, beneath the filler cords and above working cord four. Pull and tie all active strings. It is a knot in a square facing right.

SPIRAL STITCH

The Spiral Stitch, also known as a Half Knot Spiral or a Half Knot Sinnet, is a set of half knots for spiral stitch formation. It is a decorative stitch that will be of great importance to your group. The spiral stitch requires at least four strings, two functioning strings, and two filler cords, although it may have more. Such strings are internally labeled 1−4 and shift from left to right. Strings one and four are the active strings, and the filler cords are cords two and three. Such instructions explain how to create a spiral stitch on the left side, but you could also begin on the right-hand side and use half knots on the correct side. Take job cord one and push it over your filler cords to the right just under operating cord four.

Push working cord four to the west, move under the cords of the filler but over your working cord one. Remove all operating cords and stretch the cords around the filler. Hold the same direction as before, allowing further half ties. The cords will continue spiraling as you operate.

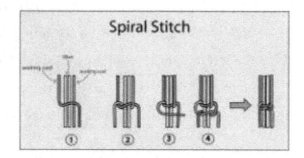

CLOVE HITCH

In your ventures, the Clove Hitch, sometimes known as a Double Half Hitch, generates row. Sometimes we can use verticality, horizontality, or diagonality.

A Horizontal Clove Hitch is a series of knots that run through your macramé project. The first chord in the knot is your filler rope, and the remainder of your cords are functioning cables. Take the left cord and place your filler cable horizontally over the other strands. To create a counter-clockwise circle, take your next cord (the first functioning cord) and carry it forward and then up and across the filler cord towards your left. Take your same cord and take it up, though and across the circle, to the right of your first knot. Two ties will now lie next to each other. That is a hook tie parallel to the clove. Undo the knots of the clove hook using your next operating rope along the same filler string. Continue to build the ties before you have the knot or pattern that you seek.

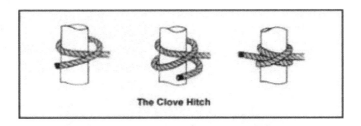

The Clove Hitch

For your project, a Diagonal Clove Hitch produces a set of diagonal ties. Take the chord at the left and place the filler chord diagonally between the other strings. Follow measures two through four of the horizontal clove hitches, going diagonally rather than straight through. Repeat before you have your perfect feel.

OVERHAND KNOT

An Overhand Knot is a simple knot that ties together multiple cords. Different cables may be used or even one cable. Stretch the string around a circle. Move the ends of your strings to close around the coil.

GATHERING KNOT

Also known as a Wrapping Knot, the gathering knot is a closure knot that binds cords together. You can also find these at the end of the plant hangers for macramé. This knot comprises two functioning strings; the remaining strings are going to work as filler cords. You need to take a different cord length (it is going to be your working cord) and build a lengthy loop (u-shaped) above the filler cord ring, with the loop facing downwards.

Beginning below the functioning cord's top-end—which points upwards—wrap it across your filler cords and your string. Make sure you keep the loop exposed for a while. Move the wrapping string end into the loop on the bottom of your wrappings. Pick up one end of your cord—that's stuck out upwards—that will put the rope under your wraps. Draw through the wraps before the coil is enclosed. The knot inset is complete. To get a smooth finish, cut both ends of your working cord if you wish.

CHAPTER 4. MACRAMÉ PROJECTS: PLANT HANGERS

MACRAMÉ PLANT HANGER (BEGINNER)

Description: Plant hanger of 2 feet and 5.5 inches (75 cm)

Knots: Square knot, alternating square knot, a half knot, and gathering knot.

Supplies:

- Cord: 10 strands of a cord of 18 feet and 0.5 inches (5,5 meter), 2 strands of 3 feet and 3.3 inches (1 meter)

- Ring: 1 round ring (wood) of 1.6 inches (4 cm) diameter

- Container: 7 inches (18 cm) diameter

Directions (step-by-step):

1. Fold the 10 long strands of cord in half through the wooden ring.

2. Tie all (now 20) strands together with 1 shorter strand with a gathering knot. Hide the cut cord ends after tying the gathering knot.

3. Make a square knot using all cords: use from each side 4 strands to make the square knot; the other 12 strands stay in the middle.

4. Divide the strands into 2 sets of 10 strands each. Tie a square knot in each set using 3 strands on each side (4 strands stay in the middle of each group).

5. Divide the strands into 3 sets of 6 strands for the outer groups and 8 strands for the group in the middle. Tie a square knot in each set using 2 strands on each side.

6. Divide the strands into 5 sets of 4 strands each and make a square knot with each set.

7. Continue with the 5 sets. In the 2 outer sets, you tie 4 square knots, and in the 3 inner sets, you tie 9 half knots.

8. Using all sets tie 7 alternating square knots by connecting two strands in each set with the right two strands of the set to it. In the first, third, fifth, and seventh row, you are not using the 2 outer strands on each side.

9. Repeat steps 7 and 8. In repeating step 8 you tie 5 alternating square knots instead of 7 alternating square knots.

10. To help you with the steps, number the strands from left to right, numbering them no.1 to no. 20.

11. With the 4 middle strands (no. 9 to 12) you make 14 square knots.

12. Make a square knot with the set of 4 strands no. 3 to 6 and the set of 4 strands no. 15 to 18.

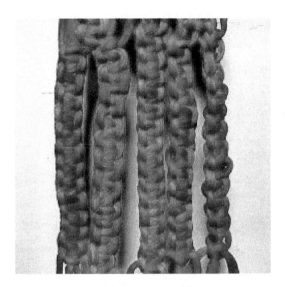

13. Divide the strands into 4 sets of 4 strands (ignore the set with the 14 square knots in the middle) and tie 12 square knots in each set.

14. Dropdown 2 inches (5 cm).

15. Make 5 sets in the following way and tie in each set a square knot:

    a. Set 1 consists of strands no. 5, 6, 1 and 2

b.   Set 2 consists of strands no. 3, 4, 9 and 10

c.   Set 3 consists of strands no. 7, 8, 13 and 14

d.   Set 4 consists of strands no. 11, 12, 17 and 18

e.   Set 5 consists of strands no. 19, 20, 16 and 15

16. Drop down another 2 inches (5 cm), no knots. This is the moment to place your chosen container/bowl into the hanger to make sure it will fit. If you need to leave more space without knots to fit your container, you can do so.

17. Gather all strands together and then tie a gathering knot with the left-over shorter strand. Trim all strands at different lengths to finish your project.

MACRAMÉ PLANT HANGER (INTERMEDIATE)

Description: Plant hanger of 4 feet and 3 inches (1,30 meter)

Knots: Square knot, alternating square knot, a half knot, alternating half hitch, gathering knot.

Supplies:

- Cord: 8 strands of cords of each 26 feet and 3 inches (8 meters), 1 short strand of cord
- Wooden Ring: 1 round ring (wood) of 1,6 inches (4 cm) diameter
- Container/Flowerpot: 7 inches (18 cm) diameter

Directions (step-by-step):

1. Fold 8 strands of cord, the long ones, in half over and through the ring. Now you have 16 strands of cord in total. Group them in sets of four strands.

2. Tie 4 square knots on each set of four strands.

3. Dropdown 3.15 inches (8 cm).

4. Tie 4 strands in each set with the right two of the set to it. Repeat on each of the 4 sets.

5. Dropdown 4.3 inches (11 cm).

6. Repeat step 4, starting with the 2 right strands this time.

7. Take 2 strands of 1 set and make 10 alternating half hitch knots. Repeat for the 2 left strands of that set. Repeat for all sets.

8. Dropdown 3.9 inches (10 cm) and tie a row of 48 half knots on each set of four strands.

9. Take the 2 middle strands of each set and make 8 alternating half hitch knots. You leave the 2 strands on the side of the set as they are (without knots).

10. Tie a row of 30 half knots on each set of four strands.

11. Use a new short strand of cord to make a gathering knot around all strands.

12. Cut off and fray the ends as desired.

MACRAMÉ PLANT HANGER (ADVANCED)

Description: Plant hanger of 2 feet and 5.5 inches (75 cm)

Knots: Square knot, alternating square knot, crown knot, gathering knot, and overhand knot.

Supplies:

- Cord: 4 strands of the cord of 13 feet and 1.5 inches (4 meters), 4 strands of 16 feet and 4.8 inches (5 meters), 2 strands of 3 feet and 3.4 inches (1 meter)
- Ring: 1 round ring (wood) of 1.5 inches (4 cm) diameter
- Beads: wooden beads
- Cristal Bowl/Container: 7 inches (18 cm) diameter

Directions (step-by-step):

1. Fold the 8 long strands of cord (4 strands of 13 feet and 1.5 inches and 4 strands of 16 feet and 4.8 inches) in half through the wooden ring.

2. Tie all (now 16) strands together with 1 shorter strand with a gathering knot. Hide the cut cord ends after tying the gathering knot.

3. Divide the strands into 4 sets of 4 strands each. Each set has 2 long strands and 2 shorter strands. Tie 5 Chinese crown knots in each set. Pull each strand tight and smooth.

4. Tie 8 square knots on each set of four strands. In each set, the 2 shorter strands are in the middle and you are tying with the 2 outers, longer strands.

5. Tie 15 half square knots with each set.

6. Dropdown 5.5 inches (14 cm), no knots, and tie an alternating square knot to connect the left two cords in each set to it.

7. Dropdown 3.15 inches (8 cm) and tie an alternating square knot with 4 strands again.

8. Dropdown 1.5 inches (4 cm). Place your chosen container/bowl into the hanger to make sure it will fit, gather all strands together and then tie a gathering knot with the left-over shorter strand. Add a bead to each strand end (optional). Tie an overhand knot in each strand and trim all strands just below the overhand knots.

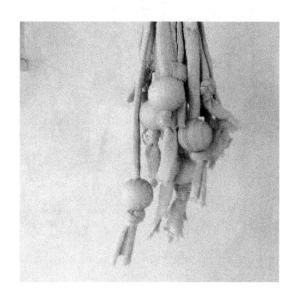

CHAPTER 5. MACRAMÉ PROJECTS: HANGING OBJECTS

CIRCLE WALL HANGING

This multifunctional, large-scale wall hanging can also be used as a small rug. Just a few basic knots are used to create the distinctive form of the piece, and you can change the color of the rope to suit your decor. If you intend to use the piece as a rug, jute makes a practical alternative to cotton rope.

Materials:

- 158.4m (527ft) length of 8mm (5/16in) rope
- Metal rings: one 6cm (23/8in); one 29cm (113/8in); one 55cm (22in); one 65cm (251/2in)

Knots and Techniques:

- Reverse Lark's Head Knot
- Square Knot
- Double Half Hitch
- Half Knot Spiral
- Fraying

Preparation:

1. Cut forty-eight 3m (10ft) lengths of 8mm (5/16in) rope
2. Cut twenty-four 60cm (231/2in) lengths of 8mm (5/16in) rope

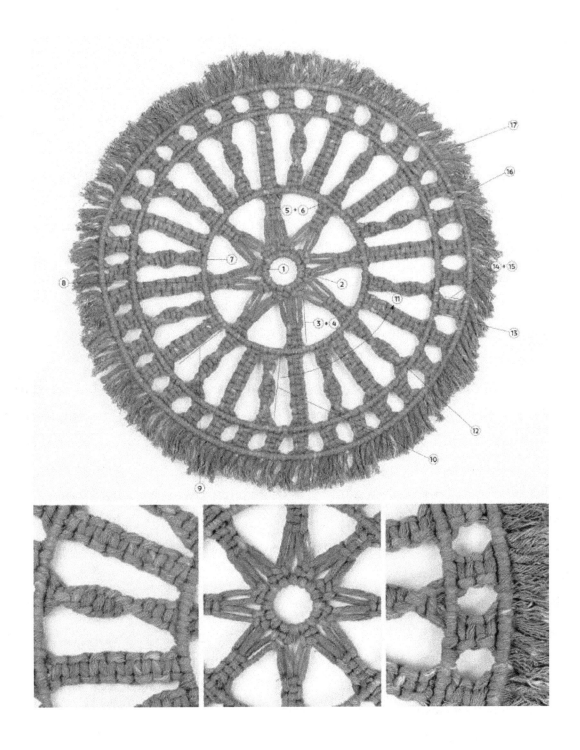

Method:

1. Mount sixteen 3m (10ft) lengths of rope onto the 6cm (23/8in) metal ring using reverse lark's head knots so that the mounted rope covers the ring. Place the ring on a flat surface so that the cords radiate out from the ring.

2. Directly beneath the ring, tie eight square knots around the diameter of the ring.

3. Alternate cords, drop down 4cm (11/2in), and tie a row of eight square knots, keeping the ring flat on the work surface and the cords radiating out from the ring.

4. Tie another eight square knots directly beneath.

5. Place the 29cm (113/8in) metal ring on top of the cords, ensuring it is evenly spaced from the first ring all the way around. This is now to be used as the holding cord.

6. Tie the cords onto the ring with double half hitches, ensuring that each of the cord groups is evenly spaced around the ring.

7. To cover the ring in between the cord groups, mount four 3m (10ft) lengths of rope with reverse lark's head knots in each of the eight spaces, using all the thirty-two remaining 3m (10ft) lengths.

8. Directly beneath the ring, tie twenty-four square knots around the diameter of the ring.

9. Take four adjacent cords beneath one of the square knots tied in step 8 and work six more square knots to create a sinnet of seven square knots with no spaces in between.

10. Take the next four cords and create a half-knot spiral net made with twelve half knots.

11. Repeat steps 9 and 10 to continue this pattern around the ring, alternating square knot, and half knot spiral sinnets.

12. Place the 55cm (22in) metal ring on top of the cords, ensuring it is evenly spaced from the second ring all the way around. This is now to be used as the holding cord. Tie the cords onto the ring with double half hitches and ensure the sinnets are evenly spaced around the ring.

13. Mount the twenty-four 60cm (231/2in) lengths of rope onto the ring, one in each of the spaces between the sinnets, using reverse lark's head knots.

14. Directly beneath the ring, tie thirty-six square knots around the diameter of the ring.

15. Tie another thirty-six square knots directly beneath the previous row.

16. Place the 65cm (251/2in) metal ring on top of the cords, ensuring it is evenly spaced from the third ring all the way around. This is now to be used as the holding cord. Tie the cords onto the ring with double half hitches.

17. Trim the cords to 6cm (23/8in) and fray.

HANGING TABLE

Give your living area a unique focal point with this truly amazing hanging table. While it can be used to display lighter ornaments, all eyes will be on the macramé itself. The hanging 'chain' is created from Chinese crown knots, and a beautiful square knot picot design has been used for the hanging straps. Please note: to hang the table, a hook must be inserted into a ceiling beam with a minimum weight-bearing capacity of 10kg (22lb).

Materials:

- 147m (482ft) length of 5mm (1/4in) rope
- Metal rings: one 6cm (23/8in); one 9cm (31/2in)
- 30cm (1ft) length of 2.5mm (1/8in) cotton twine
- 40–60cm (155/8–231/2in) circular tray of your choice

Knots and Techniques:

- Wrapped Knot
- Chinese Crown Knot
- Double Half Hitch
- Square Knot
- Alternating Square Knot Pattern
- Square Knot Picot Design
- Overhand Knot
- Fraying

Preparation:

1. Cut sixteen 9m (291/2ft) lengths of 5mm (1/4in) rope
2. Cut two 1.5m (5ft) lengths of 5mm (1/4in) rope

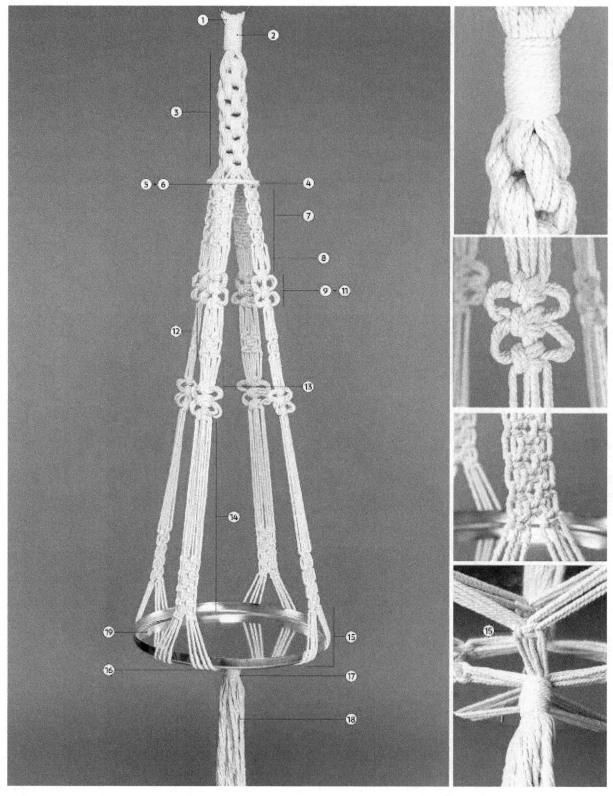

Method:

1. Mount the sixteen 9m (29 1/2 ft) lengths of rope onto the 6cm (2 3/8 in) metal ring by folding them in half over the inside of the ring.

2. Using a 1.5m (5ft) length of rope, secure the cords together with a 5cm (2in) wrapped knot.

3. Separate the cords into four groups of eight cords and tie six Chinese crown knots.

4. Directly beneath the Chinese crown knots, place all the cords inside the 9cm (3 1/2 in) metal ring. The metal ring sitting horizontally is now to be used as the holding cord. Keeping the ring level at all times, tie double half hitches with all cords onto the ring.

5. Secure the ring in place by tying a row of eight square knots directly beneath the ring.

6. Separate the cords into four groups of eight cords. Each group now becomes a sinnet. Repeat steps 7–14 for each sinnet.

7. Tie eight rows of alternating square knots.

8. Dropdown 5cm (2in) and tie a square knot using four filler cords and two working cords on either side. This is an 8-cord square knot.

9. Dropdown 3cm (1 1/8 in) and tie another 8-cord square knot.

10. Slide the square knots up the filler cords to create a square knot picot design.

11. Dropdown 5cm (2in) and tie three rows of alternating square knots.

12. Repeat steps 8–11.

13. Dropdown 27cm (10 5/8 in) and tie nine rows of alternating square knots.

14. Alternate cords by taking four cords from each adjacent sinnet and bringing them together. Dropdown 22cm (8 5/8 in) and tie an 8-cord square knot (so that each sinnet is joined to the one next to it with an 8-cord square knot).

15. Dropdown 7cm (2 3/4 in), gather all cords together and use the 30cm (1ft) length of cotton twine to tie a double overhand knot.

16. Cover the overhand knot with a 5cm (2in) wrapped knot using the remaining 1.5m (5ft) length of rope.

17. Trim the cords to the desired length and fray.

18. Insert the circular tray to create the tabletop.

BOTTLE HOLDER

Perfect for storage of a bottle of wine, this beautiful holder could also be used to showcase your favorite glass vase, and it could even double up as a plant hanger. It has rustic, plaited hanging straps and a sturdily wrapped handle. Made with jute, this piece perfectly complements any interior design scheme inspired by natural, earthy colors.

Materials:

- 44.3m (1461/4ft) length of 2mm (3/32in) jute
- Glass jar measuring 26cm (101/4in) high with an 8cm (31/8in) diameter base

Knots and Techniques:

- Chinese Crown Knot
- Square Knot
- Overhand Knot
- Wrapped Knot
- Plaiting

Preparation:

1. Cut sixteen 2.5m (81/4ft) lengths of 2mm (3/32in) jute
2. Cut one 4m (131/4ft) length of 2mm (3/32in) jute
3. Cut one 30cm (1ft) length of 2mm (3/32in) jute

f

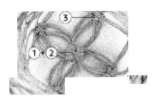

Method:

1. Divide the sixteen 2.5m (81/4ft) lengths of jute into two groups of eight cords and lay each group down on a flat surface so that they cross over at the center.

2. Tie a Chinese crown knot to secure the two groups of cord together. You now have four bundles of cord radiating out from the Chinese crown knot center—this is the start of the base of the bottle holder.

3. Bring four cords from one bundle together with four cords from its adjacent bundle, so you have a group of eight cords. Dropdown 3cm (11/8in) from the middle of the Chinese crown knot and tie an 8-cord square knot using four filler cords and two working cords on either side.

4. Repeat step 3 until you have a total of four 8-cord square knots around the center point.

5. Alternate cords as in step 3, leave a gap of 3cm (11/8in) and tie another row of four 8-cord square knots.

6. Continuing to alternate cords and leaving 3cm (11/8in) gaps in between each row, create six more rows of 8-cord square knots. (Once a cup-like shape begins to form, which should happen by about the third row, you can turn your glass jar upside down, place your cords over it and continue tying.)

7. Bring eight cords from one 8-cord square knot together with eight cords from the one adjacent to it. Dropdown 3cm (11/8in) and tie a 16-cord square knot using eight filler cords and four working cords on either side.

8. Repeat step 7 on the remaining two 8-cord square knots.

9. You now have two 16-cord square knots, one on either side of the design, and these are the starting points for making the hanging straps. Working on one of the 16-cord square knots, separate the sixteen cords into groups of five and six cords, and work a tight plait 30cm (1ft) long. Plait the cords from the second 16-cord square knot in the same way.

10. To start to make the handle, overlap the ends of the plaited straps by 5cm (2in), making sure that one sits flat on top of the other. Gather together all cords and use the 30cm (1ft) length of jute to firmly tie a double overhand knot at the center of the overlapping straps.

11. Using the remaining 4m (131/4ft) length of jute, tie a wrapped knot 14cm (51/2in) long to cover the double overhand knot, which should be at the center of the wrapped knot. Trim off all excess cords.

HANGING BASKET

Alternating square knots create a beautiful net-like pattern for the basket enclosure.

Materials:

- 167m (553ft) length of 2.5mm (1/8in) rope
- 6cm (23/8in) metal ring
- Two 20cm (77/8in) cane rings

Knots and Techniques:

- Wrapped Knot
- Square Knot
- Triple Half Hitch
- Alternating Square Knot Pattern
- Overhand Knot
- Wrapping a Ring
- Mounting Techniques

Preparation:

1. Cut forty 4m (131/4ft) lengths of 2.5mm (1/8in) rope
2. Cut three 2m (61/2ft) lengths of 2.5mm (1/8in) rope
3. Cut one 1m (31/4ft) length of 2.5mm (1/8in) rope

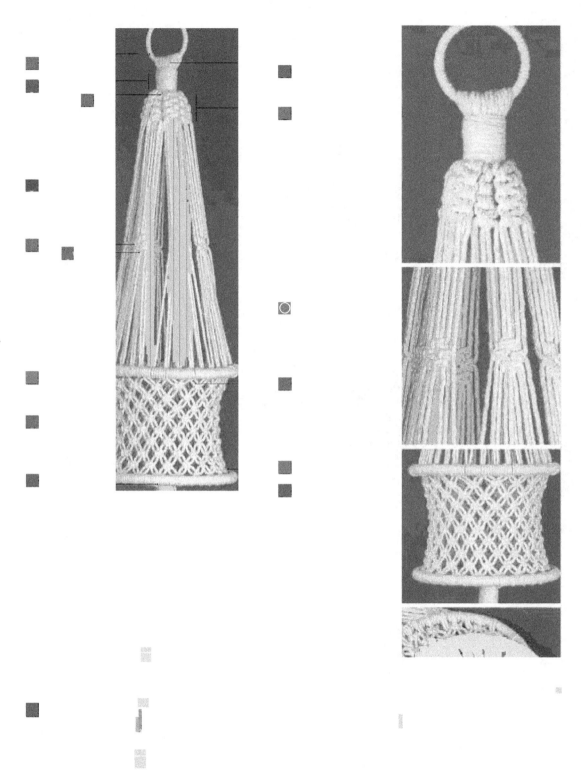

Method:

1. Wrap the 6cm (2 3/8in) metal ring with a 2m (6 1/2ft) length of rope.
2. Mount the forty 4m (13 1/8ft) lengths of rope onto the ring by folding them in half over the inside of the ring.
3. Using one of the 2m (6 1/2ft) lengths of rope, secure all cords together directly under the ring using a 3.5cm (1 3/8in) wrapped knot.
4. Directly under the wrapped knot, separate the cords into eight groups of ten cords. Each group will now become a sinnet. Repeat steps 5–8 for each sinnet.
5. Tie four 10-cord square knots using four filler cords and three working cords on each side.
6. Dropdown 17cm (6 3/4in) and use the middle six cords to tie one 6-cord square knot using four filler cords and one working cord on each side.
7. Directly beneath, alternate cords and tie two 5-cord square knots using three filler cords and one working cord on each side.
8. Directly beneath, use the middle six cords to tie another 6-cord square knot, using four filler cords and one working cord on each side.
9. Dropdown 17cm (6 3/4in) and place all of the cords inside the first of your cane rings. The cane ring sitting horizontally is now to be used as the holding cord. Tie triple half hitches with each cord onto the cane ring.
10. Secure the first cane ring by tying a row of twenty square knots directly beneath the ring.
11. Dropdown 1.5cm (5/8in), alternate cords, and tie another row of twenty square knots.
12. Continue an alternating square knot pattern for another eight rows.
13. Place all cords inside the second cane ring. The cane ring sitting horizontally is now to be used as the holding cord. Tie triple half hitches with each cord onto the cane ring.
14. Gather the rope firmly and bring it upwards until it is centered and level with the cane ring. This will create a base for the hanging basket. Secure with a double overhand knot using the 1m (3 1/4ft) length of rope.
15. Using the remaining 2m (6 1/2ft) length of rope, tie a 3.5cm (1 3/8in) wrapped knot over the top of the double overhand knot.
16. Trim the cords to the desired length.

CHAPTER 6. MACRAMÉ PROJECTS: JEWELRY

DIY MACRAMÉ BRACELET

Things you'll need:

- 4 yards of Chinese 0.5 mm Knotting Cord
- A charm or charm or connector
- an embroidery needles
- Pair of scissors
- Flat pliers (optional) for the nose
- (Optional) A lighter

Steps:

1. Start by cutting two 30-inch, two 20-inch, and one 10-inch length of the knotting cord. Pull the string through the ring, place it over the ring, and pull the remainder of the string via the loop. Fold the 20-inch section in half. Repeat the step on the other side of the ring. It will anchor these strands and remain attached.

2. The 30-inch cord is positioned under the two middle strands. Over the center strands and below the left string, fold the right string. Under the right and center strands and through the loop on the right side, pull the left cord.

3. Slide the knot up to the top and yank rigidly.

4. By bending the left cord over the center strands and under the correct cord, finish the 2nd half of the square knot. Under the left and middle threads and through the loop on the left side, squeeze the right cord.

5. Pull and repeat the phases firmly-left, right, left, right. Until the desired length is reached, commence knotting. Keep in mind that about half an inch will be taken up by the clasp.

6. Thread one of the cords on a needle to complete the knots and sew the middle of the 3-4 knots along the rear side. Through the dense knots, pliers will help pull the needle.

7. On the other cord, follow the same move.

8. Trim away the excess until all knotting cords have been sewn together. To seal it for extra hold, save the offcuts and melt the tips with a lighter. In the second half of the bracelet, repeat the same specific step.

9. Shape the bracelet into a loop and cross the center strands to create a moving closure. Using scraps to bind the cords at either end together temporarily.

10. Take the 10-inch cord under the strands and concentrate it. Start tying square knots pretty much the same way you completed the bracelet.

11. At about half an inch, halt and sew the knotting cords through the closure's backside. Remove the interim ties.

12. The two sets of middle strands are the bracelet's flexible ties now. Alter and link each end into knots to fit the wrist. Trim the excess away.

13. Your knotted customizable bracelets are done.

DIY MACRAMÉ RHINESTONE BRACELET

Things you'll need:

- 0.8 mm Chinese Knotting Thread 3 Yards

- 1 large button made of rhinestone

- 1 tiny rhinestone button

- 1 needle used for embroidery

- Tape

- Scissors

- Lighter

Steps:

1. Split one 20" string and one 60" string into the knotting cord.

2. Fold in half the short cord and tape the pleat to a working surface. The long cord must be centered beneath the two middle strings. Consider folding the right-side cord over the center strings and beneath the left-side cord.

3. Tug the left cord below the right and center strands and into the knot on the right thread. Pull firmly and pull the lump up and form a trivial circle/loop. The loop/circle must be able to wiggle over the tiny rhinestone button.

4. Proceed the square knot by bending the left string over the center strands and under the right string. Squeeze the right string underneath the left and center strings thru the thread on the left-hand side.

5. Jam firmly and repeat the steps from left to right and again left to right. At the halfway point, stop knotting.

6. Onto the 2 center strands, connect the large rhinestone button. Continue knotting. To verify the fit, evaluate the bracelet around the wrist. From the first to the last knot, the fit must be very close.

7. To complete the bracelet, weave each of the side clamps against a needle and knit up the center through 2-3 knots across the backside. Through the tight knots, pliers may help wrench the needle.

8. Then onto the middle strands, attach the small rhinestone button. Connect the central strands into the same loops around the backside.

9. Snip all 4 strings, leaving about 5 millimeters relaxed. Ignite the edges and push the melted ends onto the rear side of the bracelet with the end of the lighter to enclose it.

10. And your bracelet is ready.

11. If the bracelet is a little too fit, you can continuously give it a quick yank—it will extend out a bit.

DIY SLIDING KNOT BRACELET

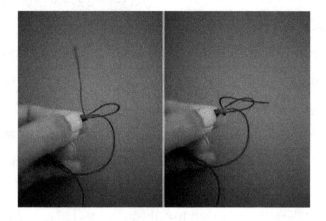

Things you'll need:

- Evil eye or charm of Hamsa
- Chinese Knotting Thread, 12 inches
- Scissor
- Lighter

Steps:

1. Connect 4 inches of the cord into one of the charms' ends. To build a zig-zag, turn 2 inches of cord back into itself and then again.
2. Over the parallel strings, fold an inch of the tip backward. Coil the string into the loop three times.
3. Connect the tip into the left loop's opening.
4. To the right, pull the coil and draw the tip until the knot is firm. By slipping it toward the center of the charm, check the customizable knot. It will trim the excess cord later.
5. Thread the cord's other end into the charm's opposite side to build the same zig-zag.
6. Coil the edge three times through all the cords and loop the tip around the loop.
7. To the right, shift the coil and draw the tip until the knot is secure. Trim both sides, leaving 2-3 mm or thereabouts.
8. For a lighter, melt the edges.
9. Your bracelet is finished. And you're safe from the evil eye now.

DIY GOLD TUBE BRACELET

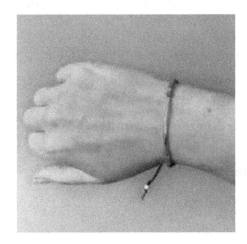

For single gold tube bracelets that are customizable, you'll need:

- A curved 2 mm x 38 mm noodle tube bead
- 0.5 mm Chinese knotting cord 2 feet
- A needle for embroidery
- 2 beads of spacer

Steps:

1. Begin by cutting two 12-inch pieces of the knotting cord. Thread into one of the strands with a gold noodle tube bead and bind the ends.
2. And now, the slipping closure is all that's left! Slide the 2nd string over the overlapping ends, like the macramé bracelet, and start binding square knots. Fold over the lowest cord with the top cord.
3. And pull the top cord through the loop into a knot under both the bottom and center alternating strands.
4. Repeat on the right side of the same step.
5. Continue to create knots about 5−6 more.

6. Thread one of the cords on a needle to complete the knots and sew the middle of the 2–3 knots around the backside. Through the tight knots, pliers will help relieve the needle.

7. Trim the extra cord away.

8. Into each loop, thread two gold spacer beads and bind the tips into a knot. Uh, Trim.

9. You're done with your customizable and colorful bracelets.

For a gold tube bracelet with a leather wrap, you'll need:

- 7-8 curved noodle tube beads 3 mm x 50 mm

- 1 yard of 1.5 mm cord in leather

- 2 crimps on the ends of the cord

- 1 tiny clasp of a spring or lobster

- A pair of pliers with a chain nose

Steps:

1. At the end of the cord, put one end of the leather string into the crimp. To tie the leather cord, grab a pair of chain-nose pliers and pinch the middle section of the end cap.

2. Thread on beads of 7–8 gold noodle tubes.

3. To gauge the correct size, loop the bracelet across the wrist. On the second end cap, trim it and crimp it.

4. Open the jump ring attached to the clasp using the pliers and link it to one of the end caps.

5. Wrap it, close it, and your bracelet is done.

6. Layer and enjoy.

DIY BRAIDED BEAD BRACELET

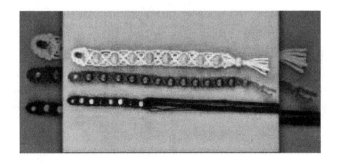

Things you'll need:

- 1.5 yards of a cord of waxed linen
- Size 50–70 8 / o Seed Beads
- A two-hole 10–13 mm button
- Scissor

Steps:

1. The waxed linen cord may be sliced into 26" and 19" sections.
2. Half-fold the longer strand. Place one side of the shorter strand with the longer strand on both ends. Fold the spare over the top of the folded component to create two parallel loops.
3. Tie a knot down from the loops for around half an inch. Snip off the fourth additional strand, leaving 3 equivalent strands similar in length.
4. Begin to braid the threads. Braid in the beads after only an inch or so. Into the outer left strand, tie a bead.
5. Place the bead against the braid's base, and cross over the center of the left strand. Thread the bead onto the right outer string now. Drive it onto the braid and crossover base.
6. At the base of the braid, keep a finger, keeping the beads in their place, and keep the braid close. On beads, begin threading until each string is crossed over.

7. Complete the bracelet by adjusting it against the wrist with another inch of plaited thread. Connect the knot.

8. Thread on a button of two holes-two strands via one hole and one string through the other. With another knot, protect it.

9. Only trim the end.

10. Your bracelets are finished! Try using waxed linen and beads in varying colors.

CHAPTER 7. MACRAMÉ PROJECTS: INDOOR ITEMS

The perfect way to add Boho flair to your space is through DIY macramé projects. It often helps you pay less, and best of all, they will make perfect gifts for your loved ones. No matter what you're looking for, whether it's a personalized gift idea for your mom on Mother's Day or for your partner on Valentine's Day or anniversary, these Macramé projects are always exceptional for the indoors.

MACRAMÉ WALL AND DOOR HANGINGS

A hung macramé wall is a simple DIY project that will bring a personalized touch to every space within your house. This tutorial can allow you to build a wall hanging with several fun designs, including spirals and triangles. Do not worry about changing it up to make it your own.

Notwithstanding how it sounds, this straightforward project only requires one or two hours to finish. It always comes together easily, and you will notice many ways to introduce your theme. The knots that you are going to use for hanging this macramé wall contain Lark's Head Knot, Spiral Knot, and Square Knot. By reading the instructions mentioned here on how to macramé, you can learn how to tie all those knots.

Requirements

- Cotton Macramé Cord (61 m or 200 feet)
- Wood Dowel (3/4 "diameter, 24" long)

- Scissors

How to Create

The wooden dowel should not be in such exact proportions, so choose any scale you want in place of the wooden dowel as long as you can accommodate all the ropes over it. If you choose to give it a more natural look, a tree branch around the same size may be used.

1. Make your wooden dowel a hanger.
2. A macramé string attached to a wooden dowel with scissors next to it.
3. Cut a three-foot (one meter) length of macramé thread. Add each end of the cord to the wooden dowel on both sides.
4. Macramé thread sliced into pieces, utilizing a pair of scissors.
5. Split the macramé string into 12 rope pieces, which are 15 feet wide (4.5 meters).
6. It may seem like a ton of rope, but knots take up more string than you thought. There is no way to make the rope thicker if you need to, but taking further is easier than utilizing.
7. Fold one of the macramé cords in two and then tie it to the wooden dowel utilizing the Lark's Head Knot. Likewise, add such strings.
8. Take the first four cords and create a spiral stitch to the left (also called a half-knot sinnet) by making 13 half knots.
9. Utilizing the next package of four ropes to perform another 13, half knots spiral stitch. Keep operating in 4-cord parties. You should have six spiral stitches when you finish.
10. Measure about two inches Bottom in spiral stitch from the last knot. It is where the next knot, the square knot, would be placed.
11. Create a right-facing square tie, utilizing the first four strings. Go across this row, rendering the correct square knots faced. Do everything possible so that both are placed horizontally together. You are going to wind up with six square knots in the band.
12. Then it is time to start decreasing the square knots, and we can get a "V" knots form.

13. Leave the two cords first, and the two cords last secure. Create square ties facing each set of four to the right. You will also have a second row of unknotted two first and two last strings and five square knots.

14. It does not matter if you spread these out; just hold them for each row and each other.

15. You must cut out the first four cords for the third section and the remaining four cords. You are going to have four knots in the square.

16. Take out six cords at the start for the fourth section and six cords at the top. You are going to get three knots in the line.

17. In the fifth section, at the top, you can cut out eight cords and, in the end, eight cords more. Now you should have two knots in the line.

18. You will cut out ten cords at the start for the sixth and final section and ten cords at the top. This will leave you with four cords to make a final knot in the square.

19. Time to bring on some square ties. We will be growing them this time to shape a triangle, like an upside-Bottom "V."

20. Take out the first eight and last eight cords to the first row of this segment. You are going to create two knots in the line.

21. Leave out six cords at the beginning and end in the third section. Within this row, you should have three knots within the line.

22. Take out four cords at the beginning of the fourth section and four at the top. You are going to have four knots in the square.

23. Take out at the start two cords in the fifth section and the last two cords. Now in this row, you should have five knots in the line.

24. Use all the cords to make knots in the last row. With this row, you should have six knots in the line.

25. Time to put a good trim on your macramé board. Leave some room beneath the final row (six to eight inches or so). Utilizing the scissors to the right through the strings.

26. You may keep it as if it is, connect any pins, fray the ends, or make basic knots overhand as above.

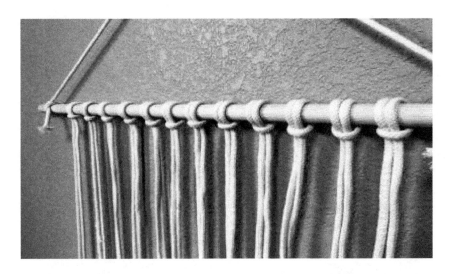

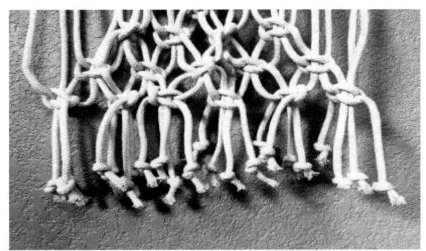

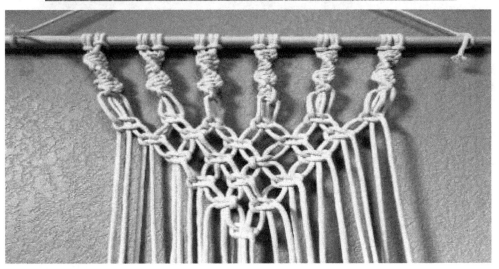

91

DREAM CATCHER

This surrealistic macramé creation is perfect to create as a treat for somebody dear to you.

Requirements

- Feathers
- A 4" brass ring
- 6 yards of any specific cording kind, 2 mm in size
- 15 Pony beads

How to Create

1. Attach the brass ring to one edge of the cording.

2. Loop the cording around the chain, ensuring sure to pull firmly after each loop. To begin the next web row, simply loop the cord around the first cord and drop. Start looping until the target size is the gap in the middle.

3. You can attach the beads anywhere in the pattern when creating the dream catcher. Loop the cord just before inserting the bead and then move the cord into the bead. The bead is then placed within the design's site.

4. When the site design is growing, you can use the cording to cover the frame—utilizing a Double Knot to lock one end of the chain. Cover the ring length with the cording and then connect the ends to be stable.

5. Split a 6-8-inch-long piece of cording. Attach the beads anywhere you want, and make sure you attach a Double Knot after the last bead. Move a feather via the beads before snugly placed. Utilizing a Double Knot to tie the rope to the loop.

6. Utilize an outer sheath of 6-inch cording, attached to the base of the dream catcher, to mount the finished product.

MACRAMÉ TABLE RUNNER

All you need to learn is three easy knots, and you have a charm layer that works every season. When you are acquainted with the knots shared here, you can tailor your table runner to suit your specific table duration or alter it entirely and build a hanging macramé wall.

Supplies:

- 12" Holden Multiple
- 22 strands of 16" cotton rope loops measuring 3 mm
- Hooks over the entrance
- 2m of cotton dowel hanger twine
- Scissors

1. Attach cotton twine to either end of your dowel or hang it from your hooks above the entrance. Fold in half the first 16' rope loop and build the head knot of a lark over the dowel.
2. Keep applying the Lark's Head Knot to each 16' string of rope until you have 22 overalls. That will send you 44 functioning strands.
3. Move the outer right rope over the top of all the other ropes (to the left) and drape the end to the hook at your entrance. This will be the basis for the next row of knots called a half hitch, which

creates a horizontal row—Utilizing the second rope to attach a single knot across the cord that you've already stretched over so that it's around 6" below the dowel.

4. Form a second knot over the base strand utilizing the same thread. It is considered a semi-hitch knot.

5. Make sure they are clear and correct.

6. Continue from outside for the second, third, and fourth rope and make another half-hitch knot, so it's tight, and so on. You are going to start looking at trends. It is a half-hitch lateral.

7. Keep linking successive knots all the way around in one knot. You do not want this to be so close that the space at the edges is drawn back.

8. Utilizing the outer four strands from the right again, and build a square knot around 1.5" below the horizontal knots rows.

9. Avoid the next four strands (five through eight) and Utilizing strands nine through 12 to form another square knot. Continue to skip four; join four before you get through all the way.

10. Beginning right again, utilizing the four strands you have missed (five through eight) and tie a square knot below the dowel around 3".

11. Keep binding four-strand missed sets in square knots until you complete the sequence.

12. Take the two outer strands out to the hand at the top. In phase seven, utilizing strands three to six to build another square knot about 11" below the horizontal row of knots. Besides, use the next four strands to construct another square knot over the last square knot, around 1.5".

13. Go all the way around, as shown. With the last two lines, you will not achieve something.

14. Follow measures three through seven to build another series of horizontal half-hitch knots beginning from the right side again.

15. Utilizing the same base strand of rope beginning from the left side and build another horizontal half-hitch row of knots around 2.5" below the previous. In this one, you are going to be operating from left to right.

16. Beginning on the left hand, build a row of square knots without missing any strands below the horizontal line of knots, around 1" away. Instead, construct a second row of square knots by missing the first two threads on the left before joining a complete row of square knots together.

It is regarded as an alternating square knot. You do not want a lot of room between those rows, and you can draw them together closely as each square knot is applied.

17. Repeat until you have a minimum of about 13 rows of alternating square knots. This portion is the core of your table runner, and anything else from this stage should echo what you have already woven above.

18. Attach another half-hitch horizontal row of knots beginning from the outer left side and making your way to the center.

19. Utilizing the same base rope to travel bottom around 2.5" to create another horizontal half-hitch series of knots that travel from right to left.

20. Skip the outer two rope strands to the right for this segment and then make a square knot, utilizing strands three to six. Skip strands from seven to ten, and use strands from 11 to 14 to tie another square knot. Repeat so for every four strands you missed. Across the left-hand side, you should find six lines.

21. Skip one and two sections on the left side and bind three to six strands into a square knot approximately 1.5" below the last set of square knots. Then miss the next four strands and finish the template for the square knots second section. It would put you on the correct side, with six additional threads.

22. Measure 11" from the last row of horizontal ties and create a square knot utilizing the right side of the outer four lines. Then bind the next four into a square knot over the last knot, around 1.5".

23. Repeat straight.

CHAPTER 8. MACRAMÉ PROJECTS: MORE INDOOR ITEMS

MACRAMÉ PILLOW

Materials:

- Macramé Cord
- Scissors
- Sewing Machine/Thread (optional)
- Pillow cover
- Attach dowel or stick tape

Measure to this pillow; you can either start with a pillow cover that you already have or make a simple pillow cover. But don't just make it yet—see first step 5.

Steps:

1. Cut the cords in! To make this pattern, you'll need 16–12-foot cords.

2. Use reverse-lark head knots to tie all 16 of your cords to your dowel.

3. The pattern for this cover is just 1 alternating square knot in the line. Leave a little gap between each knot-around half an inch as a reference point. What's more, having a bit of space makes the project go much faster.

4. Create two horizontal rows of (left-to-right, then right-to-left) or double half-hitch knots until you touch down.

5. Now that we're done with the pattern cut off the excess from the bottom but keep a little fringe

6. Now you're either going to remove your dowel or simply cut it off at step 5: How can you add this to your pillow cover?

7. Here's how to attach your macramé pattern to your pillow. Before you sew it up, if you're making a cover yourself—you're essentially going to line up the pattern to the front of your cover, leaving the cut ends a little over the top hang.

8. Lay down the pattern over the front and put the back piece on top!

9. Place the back piece over your cover and macramé template-right sides facing each other—essentially, you make a sandwich here, and the macramé is called the "meat."

10. Now just patch your pillow cover's top seam-go over the ropes too! It takes some degree of finesse, but you can.

11. Shove the macramé pattern within your pillow to stitch the rest of your cover and stitch the remaining seams as usual.

12. Flip it straight out. Now you should have your macramé pattern added to the top of your pillow (coming out from inside between the seams).

13. Take and loop a cord through your pattern.

14. Take the other hand through your pillow on the bottom... do this many times (crisscross) and knot it!

15. And it is! It's left your fringe dangling from the edges.

16. Even if the pillow cover is ready-made?

MIRROR WALL HANGING

Materials:

- Macramé Cording: 4 mm
- Mirrored octagon
- 2 inches wood ring
- Wood beads: 25 mm w/10 mm hole size
- Strong scissors.

Steps:

1. Cut 4 pieces of cording macramé into sections of 108 inches (or 3yds). Cut the strips in half and tie all four of them with a Lark's Head knot on the wood loop. Tightly and closely pull the knots. Separate two head knots from the Lark's Head knot and begin to tie them into a square knot. Start tying into the second two Lark's Head knots, two square knots. As you start the second knot of the square, loop it through one of the sides of the other two knots into a wide knot of the square. Fasten 7 square knots on both sides. Break the ends after the knots have been tied. Two strings per side and four in the center. To secure the frayed ends, apply tape to the ends of the thread.

This will make inserting the beads simpler. Congratulations. That's been the toughest part! The others are easy ties to tie and even get the sides.

2. In each of the 2 side cording lines, apply one bead. Tie a knot on both sides under the bead to keep them even. Connect the four cords in the middle to a simple or (overhand knot) about 1/14 inch below the beads. Take a cord from the center and add it to the sides of the two cords. Tie the three on both sides in a knot. Apply the mirror to the end of the knot. Add one of the three sides to the mirror's back to hold it steady. Place clear knots in all 3 side cables at the bottom left and right side of the mirror. Trim the cords again on all three sides. Return one to the back of the mirror on either side and add 2 to the front of it on each side.

3. Flip the mirror over and tie together all the cords. Flip over the mirror and loosen the knot at the front. Inside the knot, slip the back cords and straighten the knot. Cutting the cord ends up to around 14 inches. Take the ends or loose the cord and let them break. Combine the ends of the cording to fluff ends with a comb. Hang up and have fun!

100

AMAZING MACRAMÉ CURTAIN

Macramé curtains give your house the feel of that beach house look. You don't even have to add any trinkets or shells—but you can, if you want to. Anyway, here's a great Macramé Curtain that you can make!

What you need:

- Laundry rope (or any kind of rope/cord you want)
- Curtain rod
- Scissors
- Pins
- Lighter
- Tape

Instructions:

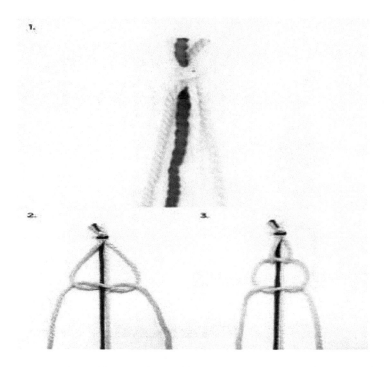

1. Tie four strands together and secure the top knots with pins so they could hold the structure down.

2. Take the strand on the outer right part and let it cross over to the left side, employing passing it through the middle. Tightly pull the strings together and reverse.

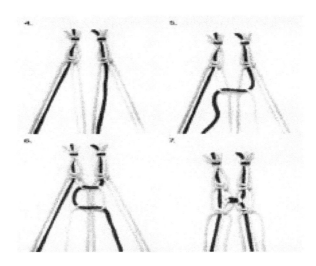

3. Repeat crossing the thread over four more times for the thread you now have in front of you. Take the strand on the outer left and let it pass through the middle and then take the right and let it cross over the left side. Repeat as needed and then divide the group of strands to the left and also to the right. Repeat until you reach the number of rows you want.

4. You can now apply this to the ropes. Gather the number of ropes you want—10 to 14 is okay, or whatever fits the rod, with good spacing. Start knotting at the top of the curtain until you reach your desired length. You can burn or tape the ends to prevent them from unraveling.

5. Braid the ropes together to give them that dreamy, beachside effect, just like what you see below.

6. That's it; you can now use your new curtain!

CHAPTER 9. MACRAMÉ PROJECTS: OUTDOOR ITEMS

MACRAMÉ LAWN CHAIRS

Tools and Supplies

- Lighter
- Scissors
- Crochet Hooks
- Paracord or Macramé Cord
- Metal Lawn Chair

Method

1. Use a pair of scissors to remove your chair's webbing. You may require a screwdriver as well if the webbing on your chair has been secured using screws.

2. Create a double knot on the base of your chair.

3. Bring your cord up, under the bar in the middle, then up over your frame at the top.

4. Wrap your cord, then loop it from the front part of your chair back and forth, pull it up to the top of your chair's back. Rework the steps to wrap your cord again from the bottom to the top.

5. To create a pattern on your chair, rework the same steps as you did when facing vertically; however, as opposed to last time, weave your macramé cord (or paracord) horizontally.

6. Form a knot at the tip once you are done weaving. Using a lighter, burn off the strand that is left hanging.

MACRAMÉ OUTDOOR PLANTER

Tools and Supplies

- Herb Plants
- Planter Pot
- Level
- Painter's Tape
- Screws
- Drill
- Scissors
- Hose Clamps
- Copper pipe

- Masonry Line
- Curtain Rod Brackets (2)

Method

1. Install the pipe made of copper. Get a copper pipe cut to your preferred length from your local hardware. Form a straight line against your wall using painter's tape and a level. For a field that is level hanging, use hanging brackets.

2. Use a masonry line that has been cut. Any heavy strand will get the job done; however, the masonry line is available in a variety of colors. Copper looks great with a touch of neon pink or yellow. Cut out six-string strands, ensuring that every piece is thrice your pots' length.

3. Recalibrate your hose clamp. Make the hose clamp tight around your pot's top using a screwdriver. You need to make sure that the fit is snug. Remove it from the pot when it is the correct size, then place it on a flat surface.

4. Begin to create the knots. Take one of your strands and fold it into equal parts. At your mid-point, create a loop below your hose clamp, then pull both tails through. Repeat this step with the remaining strings. Evenly space 6 strands around your clamp. Get two strands that are on opposite sides, then wrap them into a knot approximately 1½" below. Redo with each of your strands. Use the right and left strings to keep creating 1 ½" knots until you achieve your required length for the pot. You may slide the pot inside to check how many extra knot rows you have to make. When you hold up your hose clamp, it should resemble a basketball hoop.

5. Plant your herbs. Pour potting soil into your pot around the herb roots ensuring that you do not overfill. Try faux plants or succulents if you normally have a lot on your plate. Position your hose clamp around your pot, then form a knot at the base. Clip off the strands at the bottom as necessary; make it as short or as long as you want.

6. Hang the planter. Cut out 3 masonry line strands, then create knots in that length to add a little detail. You will need 2 of these. Loop the strand that is knotted below the hose clamp, then knot it on the pipe made of copper. Redo on the other side. You may find that your planter is somewhat tipsy, in which case simply adjust it so that the strands are equal on the right and left side and ensure that at least the length is exact.

MACRAMÉ FRINGE UMBRELLA

Supplies

- Sewing thread – in the or same or similar color as your umbrella
- Sewing needle
- Scissors
- Macramé cotton cord
- Outdoor umbrella

Method

Note: These steps are for making fringe for one section of the outdoor umbrella. Depending on the number of umbrella poles/sections, you will need to redo everything as many times as necessary.

1. Cut out the cord pieces: Cut out a strand of the cord to be a bit longer than a section of the umbrella. Secure the line to the two ends of your umbrella ribs

110

2. Cut out eighteen strands of macramé cord: Measure, then cut eighteen strands that are four feet in length, then connect them to the strand that is already attached to the umbrella.

3. Create square knots: Use square knots to link the strands of the macramé cord. Rework this step for 3 rows.

4. Clip off the extra pieces: Remove the curls from the fringes that are twisted. If your cord is not twisted, you are done.

MACRAMÉ PLACEMAT

Tools and Supplies

- One pair of sharp scissors
- One comb
- Metal clothes hanger
- 3-4mm of 20 x 3m thick cotton string

Method

1. Use a lark's head knot to mount twenty strings that are 3m in length onto a metal hanger. Leave out a space of two to three mm between your knots.

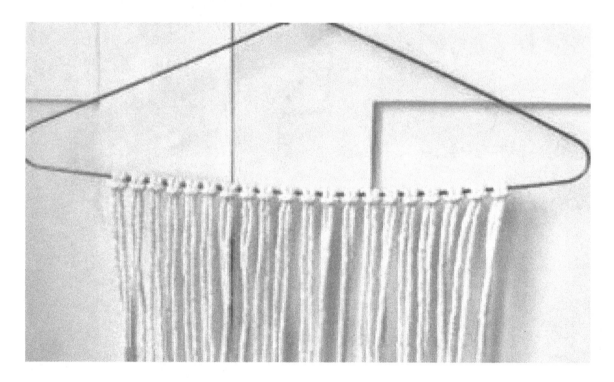

2. Leaving out a distance of five centimeters under your knots, grab four strands, then use them to create a square knot beginning from the left side. Use the four strands that follow to create another SK. Proceed until you achieve one row of ten SKs.

3. Create a row of 9 square knots. Beginning from your left side, grab strands three and four from the initial knot, then strands 2 and 1 from the one adjacent to it to create a new square knot. Proceed through the length of your row. Repeat steps two and three until you get a total of 5 square knot rows (the final row is going to have ten).

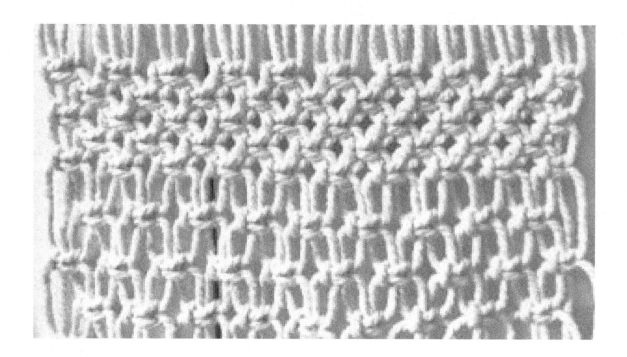

4. Leaving out a space of two to three centimeters, create a fresh row of 9 SKs. Do another row of ten square knots after leaving out a two-to-three-centimeter space.

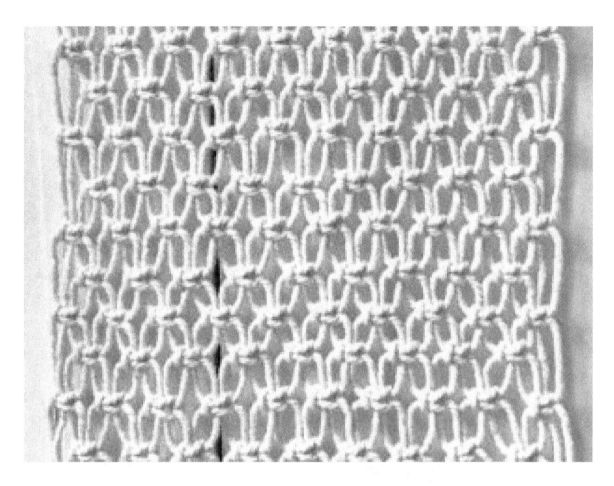

5. Repeat step four until you get a total of twelve rows, completing with one that has ten knots.

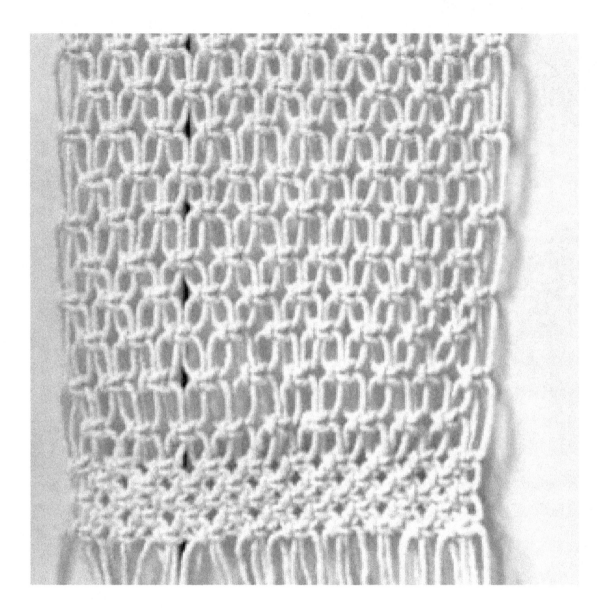

6. Create a row of ten, nine, ten, nine, and ten square knots minus any spaces in between your rows to complete the design. Remove the placemat from your hanger by clipping the lark's head knot.

7. Fold the placemat into two over the hanger, then clip the strands on either end to your preferred length, ensuring that they are all even. To finish, make a soft feathery fringe by combing the ends.

MACRAMÉ HANGING LANTERN JARS

Tools and Supplies

- Scissors
- Sticky tape
- Candles – for safety purposes, LED is best
- Jar
- String or twine

Method

1. Cut out a piece of twine that is approximately eight times the intended length. Cut out eight more twine pieces with a similar length.

2. Separate your twine pieces into two sets of 4 lengths, then spread them out, crossing each other at the middle.

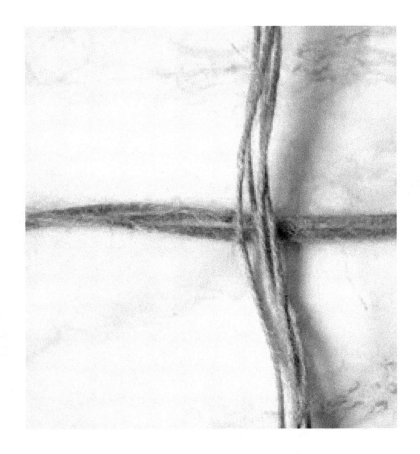

3. Thread the top of the lengths that are vertical below the horizontal ones.

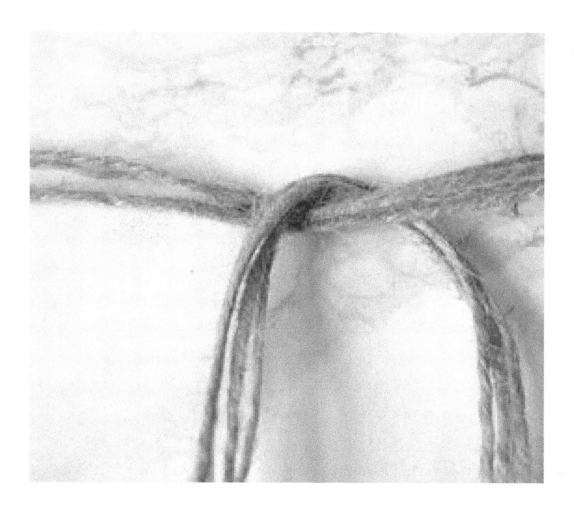

4. Cross the end on the right side of the horizontal below the vertical lengths. Cross it beyond their top to make the shape of 'S'.

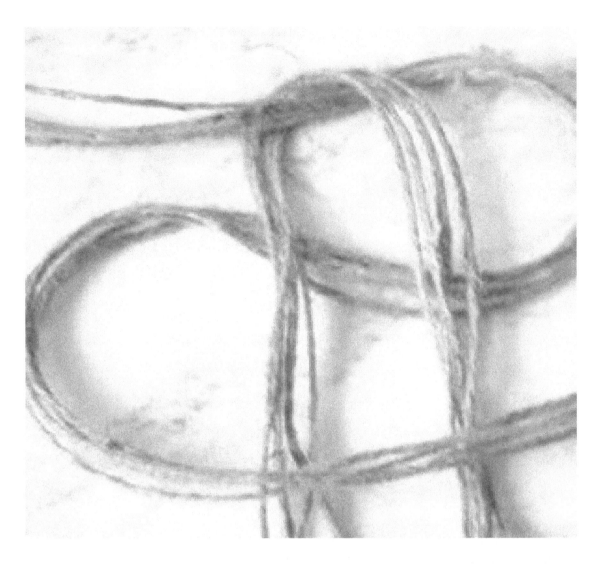

5. Grab the horizontal pieces of the lengths to the left, then pass them through the loop to your right. Pull all the ends of the strands one set at a go until you form a knot.

6. Turn to the upright side, then separate your twine strands into pairs. Knot each pair at approximately the distance from the edge to the middle of the jar.

  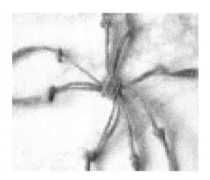

7. Turn your jar over once more upside down, then secure your lanyard knot to the middle of the base of your jar using tape. Tie the length of your right side from one of the pairs with the length on your left side from the pair adjacent to it, then repeat all around. Repeat down the length of your jar at intervals that are even until you get to the top.

 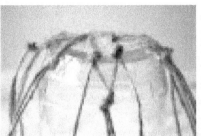 

8. Insert your candle then, create a knot from all your strands, ensuring that you leave out enough space for your jar to hang.

CONCLUSION

As we end this book, I would like to share the most common mistakes in doing macramé projects and how to fix them. They are as follows:

ERROR 1: WHEN TYING A KNOT, DOING IT IN A SLOPPY WAY

How to Fix:

1. Hold the cord under the 6-inch mark (junction) with your left hand and the cord end facing upward on top of your right hand.
2. Bend both hands inward, making sure the cords are at the same level and are under pressure before tying the knot, as shown in the picture.
3. Pull on both ends of the cord to tighten the knot before cutting off the excess part of both cords.

ERROR 2: NOT MAKING THE CORD LONGER WHEN MAKING A KNOT

How to Fix:

1. Keep tension on the knot, 1–2 inches higher than the knot itself.
2. Pull on both ends of the cord to pull it in; this will reduce any stress caused by the knot, resulting in more durability for your cord and fastening knots well.

ERROR 3: NOT USING ENOUGH TENSION WHILE TYING KNOTS AND CORDS TOGETHER

How to Fix:

1. When tying a new cord to an existing rope, tighten it under pressure, don't let it flop around loosely.
2. When adding another loop of cord to an existing rope, make sure that you pull fairly hard on all ends of both cords before joining them together.
3. When adding one or more cords to an existing cord, regulate the pressure so that both cords are under equal tension at all times.

ERROR 4: NOT USING THE RIGHT TYPE OF KNOT FOR A CERTAIN MACRAMÉ PROJECT

How to Fix:

1. Using a Granny knot for decorative purposes only and not for fastening rope together.
2. Using a Lark's Head knot for an 8-in-1 or 6-in-1 when you should have used an Overhand knot.
3. Using an Overhand knot when you should have used an Overhand Loop Knot.
4. And many others too...

HOW CAN YOU PREVENT MAKING MACRAMÉ MISTAKES?

- Read and understand the instructions carefully before starting a project.
- IMPORTANT: Do all the knots slowly and carefully, don't be in a hurry or just "wing it."
- Be enduring with yourself; this is not some kind of race, so take your time to do things properly and neatly.
- Similarly, it helps if you have somebody who is experienced in macramé nearby to assist whenever you get stuck in doing a certain knot or technique.
- Lastly, is to keep a positive attitude in doing projects. Any time you find yourself getting frustrated with how a project is going, stop, walk away and take a break from it. You can at all times come back to it later and start again when you're calm again. Remember, this is not something that you finish overnight, nor should you pressure yourself into finishing it as fast as possible since the result will be more satisfying when done properly and neatly.

Thank you for reading this book, and I hope you enjoy doing macramé!

Good Luck with Your Macramé Projects!

CPSIA information can be obtained
at www.ICGtesting.com
Printed in the USA
LVHW060107300721
694062LV00003B/96